The Black Cab Story

The Black Cab Story

Alf Townsend

The
History
Press

Published in the United Kingdom in 2009 by
The History Press
The Mill · Brimscombe Port ·
Stroud · Gloucestershire · GL5 2QG
www.thehistorypress.co.uk

Reprinted 2011

British Library Cataloguing in Publication Data
A catalogue record for this book is available from the British
Library.

ISBN 978-0-7509-4853-1

Typesetting and origination by
The History Press
Printed in China

Title and half-title page: *The New TX4, launched in
late 2006. Instead of calling it the TXIII, they called
it the TX4 to link it with the euro four emissions
ruling. It has the same body and chassis as a TXII
but is powered by a VM turbocharged diesel
engine.
(LTI Limited reproduced with permission. Fairway
and TX shape is a registered design. Fairway[TM],
TX[TM], the LTI Device, the LTI logo and the London
Taxis International logo are all trademarks of LTI
Limited.)*

CONTENTS

The whole concept of hailing a taxi in London is unique. Firstly, the 24,000-plus purpose-built vehicles are tough, sturdy, safe and have to comply with the stringent 'Conditions of Fitness' laid down by the trade's regulatory body, the Public Carriage Office (PCO). If these stringent 'Conditions of Fitness' were ever watered-down then the iconic London taxi would become extinct – undercut by cheaper people-carriers.

The floor level of the passenger compartment must not be more than 15in above ground level when the vehicle is unladen so that the punters can easily get in and out. Every cab must be wheelchair accessible and every London taxi needs to have a thorough overhaul every year before its Hackney Carriage Plate is renewed – and I mean VERY thorough! The cabbies need to

keep their vehicles immaculate at all times because teams of Carriage Office Inspectors prowl the London streets day and night

◄
Jamie Borwick, the then MD of LTI, launches the TX1 in 1997 with actress Joanna Lumley. My thanks to Jamie for letting me delve into his extensive collection. (Author's Collection)

◄◄
(London Vintage Taxi Association Collection)

Did you know?
The London taxi must have a turning circle of 25ft so it can U-turn off a central rank.

Did you know?

The reason why London taxis are so high is so that the 'toffs' didn't have to remove their tops hats!

looking for tatty cabs. These unfortunate cabs are given 'Stop-Notes' and can, and often do, cost the driver lots of dough, because the vehicle is put up on a ramp and checked over with a fine-tooth comb!

Secondly we come to the 22,000-plus drivers, the world-famous London cabbies. Love them or hate them, nobody can dispute their professionalism and knowledge of the capital. Becoming a London taxi driver is tantamount to committing oneself to a three-year course at university – maybe not the academic side but certainly the work input. Every would-be cabbie has to sign on at the PCO – with no outstanding criminal convictions – and endure what is colloquially known as 'The Knowledge'.

This entails riding around London on a moped for around three years and basically learning every one of the 25,000 streets within a 6-mile radius of Charing Cross. But it doesn't end there. You need to remember thousands of 'points' such as hospitals, clubs, theatres, hotels, restaurants, railway stations and churches. In fact you need to remember just about every destination a punter may require – even 'knocking-shops'!

The Knowledge Boy or Girl is given what is known as the 'Blue Book' when he or she signs on. This is in fact a white book containing a list of some 400 routes or 'runs' that criss-cross all over London; why it's called the Blue Book nobody knows! After learning the Blue Book inside out, the candidate will then book an 'appearance' at the Public Carriage Office for a fifteen-minute oral test. This is crunch time in front of a merciless examiner who will deliberately switch the start and finish of

each run, to ensure that the pupil hasn't been sitting at home on their backside simply map-reading! And God help you if he twigs that you have been map reading and not braving the elements out in the freezing cold on your moped. Back in my day one of the so-called shrewd-nuts proceeded to call a 'run' and turned right off Holborn Viaduct into Farringdon Street – a drop of around 50ft. He was promptly slung off the course and told not to return!

Committing yourself to the Knowledge is a long and tiring process of elimination and the drop out rate is about 70 per cent. After many months of hard learning, your brain, almost like a computer, starts storing the masses of information and suddenly you can actually see the particular street or point the examiner is asking and you eventually walk out of the office elated with a 'full house' – every question answered correctly. Now you are really on your way and in a matter of a few short months you would have completed the suburbs (now that IS map-reading) and passed the stringent driving test. You will never, ever forget the day you were finally handed the coveted Green Badge! Not least of all, gaining your Green Badge will make you a better human being. I am a classic example. Before undertaking the Knowledge, I was a bit of a scallywag, always ducking and diving and buying and selling this and that, not bothering where the stuff came from. But not after I had acquired my badge; I had sweated too long and too hard and no way was I going to risk losing it for the sake of a quick buck! So for the past forty-six years I have trod the straight and narrow – though not quite as straight as your Roman roads, mark you!

The Knowledge was first introduced way back in 1851 by Sir Richard Mayne, one of the two Police Commissioners appointed to oversee the Hackney Carriage Trade. The story goes that this came about following complaints by visitors to the Great Exhibition that cabbies did not know where they were going! I've always had a particular fascination about the way the iconic London taxi has evolved over many years and the long history of the London cabbie. As a London cabbie myself, a trade journalist for forty years – and sometime editor of trade papers – and now an author of three published books, I consider my credentials worthy of relating this intriguing story.

◄ *Scooters lined up outside 'The Knowledge Point School' in Caledonian Road, N1.*
(Author's Collection)

Even as early as in the reign of Edward V (1461–83), bylaws were drawn up in the interests of Hackneymen.

Then in 1654 an ordinance by Oliver Cromwell called 'The Regulation of Hackney Coachmen in London' was introduced basically to lay down the pattern for every subsequent Act of Parliament concerning Hackney carriage vehicles right up to the present day. The original ordinance even included the journey limit of 6 miles – which was doubled recently by former London Mayor Ken Livingstone. Many people, including many taxi drivers, believed this 6-mile limit was to ensure that the poor old horse didn't get too tired. But in fact it was linked to London's chain of defences that had been erected during the Civil War in 1642. These defences were approximately 6 miles from the City and Westminster and it was deemed as 'dangerous' for Hackney coaches to pass through. The Lord Protector was indeed the founding father of London's taxi trade!

A century before, a massive conflict of interests came about between the watermen and the rising number of Hackney coaches that were fast becoming popular. The watermen – or water taxis – had plied their trade since Anglo-Saxon times and a Royal Charter in the twelfth century gave them the right to ply for hire. They had always enjoyed a lucrative living ferrying wealthy City merchants over to the gaming houses and stews (brothels) on Bankside; then bringing them back late in the night absolutely 'legless'.

Did you know?
The word 'Hackney' derives from the Flemish term 'haquené' – a dappled grey horse which originally came from Flanders. It has nothing whatsoever to do with the London borough of the same name.

Even such luminaries as Sir Christopher Wren took a water taxi daily from his home next to the Globe Theatre on Bankside, across the river to where he was building his masterpiece, St Paul's Cathedral.

However, suddenly the watermen's lucrative living was being jeopardised – not only by the new bridges being built, but by the many businesses that were transferring to the City area. The watermen's formerly regular clientele were now sharing Hackneys from Westminster on the north side at a cheaper rate than on the boats. Not only was it cheaper, but after the building of London Bridge, it was much safer. The bridge had been constructed with many narrow arches and the watermen had to 'shoot the rapids' to get through!

This bitter and sometimes violent conflict lasted a full fifteen years, with the watermen having powerful allies. One such person was John Taylor, a former boatman and staunch supporter of the watermen. He wrote the following verse to rouse them:

'Coaches, Garroaches, Jades and
Flanders Mares, do rob us of our fares,
our wares and our tares; while we stand and
click our heels, all our profit runs away on
wheels'

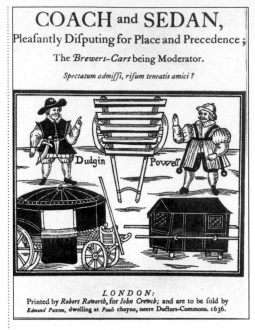

COACH and SEDAN,

Pleafantly Difputing for Place and Precedence;

The *Brewers-Cart* being Moderator.

Spectatum admiffi, rifum teneatis amici ?

Dudgin   Powell

LONDON:
Printed by *Robert Raworth*, for *Iohn Crowch*; and are to be fold by
Edmund Paxton, dwelling at *Pauls* chayne, neere Doctors-Commons. 1636.

The ever-expanding size of London eventually spelled the end for the watermen. The very first 'cab rank' was established by a Captain Bailey, a retired mariner, in 1635. Apart from dressing the drivers of his four Hackney coaches in livery and instructing them what fares to charge, most important of all, he brought them out of the courtyards and inns where they had formerly stood to be hired, then placed them one behind the other, close to the Maypole in The Strand. This rank soon attracted the attention of other hackney coachmen who flocked there seeking work. It became so popular that the modern-day cabbies still adopt the very same practice of driving slowly along a street, waiting for a space on a fully-loaded rank. This practice was very prevalent in the 'bad' old days at Heathrow Airport.

To my worthy friend the *Author*.

W Ho is it (under thirty) that beleeves
        Big-bellied-dublets, made with cloak-bag-sleeves,
That would hold pecks a peece? Wings, that belowe
The elbowe reach't? And for the better shewe,
Every large Button that went downe the brest,
(Broade as an Halfe-crowne Piece) to grace the rest?
When the short breech, not reaching past the knee,
(Crosse-garter'd at the hamme) a man might see
The Calfe apparant; with the anckle-joynts,
Not Frenchified (as now) with Aglet points
To hide their gowtie shin-bones; when the ruffe
Wide, as a Fore Coach-wheele, with starch enough,
Weare onely in the fashion? And (Friend) than
Some Coaches were in use, but no Sedan;
Nor doe I thinke, but if the Custome were
T' bee hurryed in Wheele-barrowes, t'wold appeare
(In processe) well : and they would take the wall
Of Carres, of Coaches, of Sedans and all.
And who can tell, whether 't bee now a breeding?
And may perhaps prove so in Times succeeding.
    Now when wee last discourst, close by the Mill,
Which over-lookes the Towne from Hamsted-hill,
Thou told'st mee of this project ; I then said,
This thy dispute there talk't of, and since made,
I thought would apt this age, and further vow'd,
'T should bee no sooner finish't, and alow'd.
But that I would Commend (as all may see)
It, to the World first : Next my selfe to thee.
                                                    Anonymos.

◄◄
Sedan chair and Hackney coach, seventeenth century.
(J.B. Collection)

◄
The ongoing battle between sedans and coaches even inspired poetry! (J.B. Collection)

Sala Regalis cum Curia Westmonastery, *vulgo* Westminster haall.

Hackney coaches in New Palace Yard, Westminster Hall, c. 1654.
(J.B. Collection)

'No hackneyman shall breke another's hyre'
[which in effect means don't nick another
cabbie's fare!]

The Revd Mr Garrod, commenting on these events in a letter to Lord Strafford wrote, 'Everybody is much pleased by it, for whereas coaches could be had at great rates, now a man can hail one much cheaper.'

In 1636, because of the proliferation of Hackney coaches (and possibly because of the deal he had made in 1630 with a Sir Saunders Duncombe, who hired out sedan chairs), Charles I issued a proclamation restricting the number of Hackney coaches to just fifty – and they were only allowed to pick up passengers who were travelling more than 3 miles. This confirmed suspicions that the king was acting in his own interests because this proclamation gave Sedan chairs a virtual monopoly on the short fares! But within two years, 'because the public wanted them,' the Hackney coaches were working very much as before.

Despite considerable competition from sedan chairs in the early years, the Hackney coaches became ever more powerful and influential. Parliament became more and more involved with the Hackney carriages and between 1711 and 1798 some twenty-four Acts of Parliament were passed dealing specifically with the trade. From 1662 until 1831 'apart from the years 1679 to 1683' all London's public road passenger vehicles were controlled by the Commissioners at the Hackney Coach Office in Scotland Yard and drivers were not licensed until 1843.

But too many coaches were being licensed and from 1694 up until 1815 the numbers had almost doubled to 1,200. The eighteenth century saw various Acts being passed for the limitation of the number of Hackney coaches and brought a degree of prosperity to the Hackney coachmen.

An Act of 1869 gave the Commissioner of Police other new duties to Hackney Carriages and Omnibuses. It stated the manner in which the carriages were to be fitted and furnished; the regulation of the number of persons to be carried, as well as the fixing of cab ranks, the fixing of fares and the safe custody of any property found in the vehicles.

The Hackney Coach Office was based at various addresses over the years, but as it got bigger so it required a purpose-built permanent home. This was erected in Lambeth Road in 1927 and the name was changed to the Public Carriage Office. This building existed for almost forty years until a modern new complex was opened in Penton Street, N1, in 1966. Penton Street closed at the end of 2007 and all taxi inspections were then outsourced to a private company.

Did you know?
The taxi rate of a shilling a mile first started when Charles II passed an Act for the better control of the coachmen in 1662. This 'shilling a mile' fare was not to be exceeded until 1950!

EXTERIOR OF CAB, WITH INDEX.

In between times the evolution of cab designs was becoming significant. In 1814 the introduction of 200 'Chariots' proved to be very popular and in 1823 a Mr David Davies designed the 'Cabriolet'. Twelve of these entered service and they became so popular that by 1834 their numbers had risen to 800. The Cabriolets have been immortalised in the following verse:

'In days of old when folks got tired, a Hackney Coach or a Chariot was hired; but now along the streets they roll yea, in a shay, with a cover, called a Cabriolet.'

Did you know?
The French word 'cabriolet' was shortened to 'cab' and that's what we have called them ever since!

➤
The horse is down!
(J.B. Collection)

23

The speedy Hansom cab; 'the Gondolas of London'.
(Author's Collection)

The Hackney Coach Office in Scotland Yard.
(J.B. Collection)

The four-wheeled Clarence, or 'Growler' as it was nicknamed, was introduced by the same David Davies in 1836. (J.B. Collection)

'The Hansom cabs are the gondolas of London.'

Prime Minister Benjamin Disraeli,
speaking in Parliament.

*The last of the
horse-drawn buses,
photographed in 1890.
(J.B. Collection)*

In December 1834, Joseph Hansom of Hinckley, Leicestershire, registered his Patent Safety Cab – but sold it on for £10,000 before it was manufactured. Other designers recognised defects in Hansom's cab and devised improvements which were to make this vehicle probably the most famous cab of all. In 1873, Henry Forder of Wolverhampton introduced the straight axle by cutting away the body of the cab under the passenger's seat at an angle, sloping to the floor where the passenger's feet rested. He also raised the driver's seat 7ft off the ground. The driver's weight, counterbalanced by the shafts, gave a perfectly balanced vehicle capable of reaching a heady speed of 17mph!

Did you know?

Because of the heavy congestion of London's streets, the modern London taxi's average speed is lower than the 17mph reached by the Hansom cab!

➤

*Hansom cabs on the taxi
rank in The Strand during
the Edwardian period.
(J.B. Collection)*

For the next fifty years, up until the advent of the first motor cab in the late nineteenth century, the Hansom cab and the Clarence, or 'Growler' as it was affectionately known (because of the noise it made on the cobbles), reigned supreme. It was the same David Davies, designer of the popular Cabriolet in 1823, who introduced the enclosed, four-wheeled Clarence in 1836. The growler was the plodding carriage carrying lots of luggage while the Hansom was the flyer!

Did you know?

An Act of Parliament in 1784 gave the Hackney carriage trade the sole right to use their coaches as 'hearses and mourning coaches at funerals'. An Act of 1853 gave complete control of the London Cab Trade to the Commissioner of Police and duly upset a feature writer in *The Times*, who wrote, 'no one person should have such absolute power.'

THE CABMEN'S SHELTERS

Tourists roaming the streets of London will invariably come across one of these little green huts, looking for all the world like miniature cricket pavilions, or even sheds used by the gardeners in the Royal Parks. They must ask themselves, what on earth can they be? They are in fact the famous cabmen's shelters where cabbies go to eat, meet their mates and spin a few yarns. The shelters have been around for more than a hundred years. Their long history makes for interesting reading and is a classic example of the two-faced morals and double-edged benevolence of the Victorians who seemingly accepted hardship and poverty as the norm.

The London cabmen in those far-off days worked under appalling conditions and were expected to 'sit on the box' in rain, snow, cold and wind, waiting for a fare.

It's no wonder many of them found solace from the foul weather by nipping into the local grog shop and fortifying themselves with mugs of hot cocoa – with an added nip of rum of course!

Did you know?
The old shelter in Leicester Square, donated by English actor and theatre manager Sir Squire Bancroft in 1901, was put on a lorry when the square was pedestrianised and re-sited in Russell Square where it still stands today.

➤
Elgin Avenue cab shelter, c. 1900 – now demolished. (J.B. Collection)

The story goes that in January 1875 a certain Captain Armstrong, editor of the *Globe* newspaper, who lived in St John's Wood, sent his manservant out into the blizzard that was raging at the time, to engage a cab to take him to his office in Fleet Street. Returning a full hour later with a cab, soaked to the skin, the good captain enquired of his servant why he had been so long. He was told that although there

◄◄
An old print of a cabbies' shelter. (J.B. Collection)

◄
One of the many cab shelters. (London Vintage Taxi Association Collection)

were cabs on the rank, all the cabmen had retired to a nearby grog shop to get out of the blizzard.

Captain Armstrong spoke with many of his influential friends about the fact that cabmen had nowhere to shelter from the elements. They all sympathised with the cabmen's plight and decided to donate money for the erection of a shelter adjacent to the cab rank in Acacia Road, St John's Wood – very convenient for the good captain! And so was born the London Cabmen's Shelter Fund. Many wealthy and influential people, including the Prince of Wales, later King Edward VII, subscribed to the fund. One shelter, erected in Old Palace Yard, Westminster, was paid for by Members of both Houses of Parliament, the impressive list of subscribers reading like a page from *Debrett's Peerage*!

Between 1875 and 1950, some forty-seven shelters were erected in London – all funded by a number of prominent citizens. At first the shelters had no provision for supplying meals; but by 1882 larger shelters were erected, which included a small kitchen so hot meals and drinks could be provided by the shelter-keeper. Sadly, owing to new one-way streets and road changes, many shelters were pulled down and their numbers have declined to just thirteen. But these remaining shelters have become Grade II listed buildings and are now refurbished by English Heritage, so they will live on! Many of the well known personalities of the day often frequented the cab shelters. Sir Ernest Shackleton, the famous explorer, was a regular visitor to the old shelter which originally stood at Hyde Park Corner. Prior to his last and tragic expedition, where he died at sea, the regulars presented him with a set of pipes and a pipe rack. His letter of thanks to them hung proudly on the shelter wall for many years until it was pulled down to make way for the new Piccadilly Underpass.

Many of these shelters have nicknames as well such as 'The All Nations', almost opposite the Royal Albert Hall. This got its nickname from the Great Exhibition in 1850. Then you have 'The Bell and Horns' in the middle of the road in Thurloe Place, South Kensington, and named after an old pub opposite. 'The Chapel' is in St John's Wood, while 'The Temple' is in Temple Place on the Embankment. 'The Pier', on the river by the Albert Bridge, has just been repaired after taking a direct hit from a huge lorry!

'The Temple Shelter' on Embankment. (London Vintage Taxi Association Collection)

VICTORIAN CABBIES

The following excerpt from a Government White Paper of 1895 entitled, 'The Cab and Omnibus Trades', makes for interesting reading.

The cabman's trade is one to which all sorts of men find their way. Many an educated man, who can do nothing else to earn a living, can drive – and if put to it, will seek his daily bread in this way. In the strike of 1891, it was by a man of University education that the books were kept. Cabmen have plenty of opportunity for reading the daily papers, for discussions amongst themselves, and as a result are generally up to date in general information, and often keen politicians, many being members of Radical clubs. It is these men, one hears, who are the most conservative of all on trade questions. Many again, are prominent in their temperance or religious views, and one cabman is well known as a secularist lecturer on Sunday in the parks. By constant contact with all kinds of people cabmen become very observant and often know more about those they drive than the latter imagine. Moreover, a certain confidence is reposed in their discretion and many a doubtful piece of business is transacted under their eyes – not indeed that there would be such evidence as would even warrant them making their suspicions known, but about which they have little doubt in their own minds. The relations between the cabmen and the public they drive are, on the whole, very pleasant and if

The present-day Russell Square shelter. (Author's Collection)

40

at times they become otherwise the fault is not always confined to the side of the cabmen.

HEALTH

The Cab and Omnibus Trades' White Paper went on to talk about the general medical condition of cabbies:

The principal diseases from which cabmen suffer, namely rheumatism, bronchitis and chest complaints generally, are those due to exposure to the weather. These diseases are aggravated by indulgence in strong drink, a habit which, as already indicated, is prevalent, although there are, on the other hand, not a few abstainers and a flourishing temperance society among their members. It must, however, be said that the publicity to which the men are exposed, and the fear of having their licences endorsed, prevent a good deal of excess. A cabman may drink, but he must on no account get drunk. The mortality returns, so far as they can be applied to this trade, do not give it a favourable position for longevity.

Cut out the bit about the booze and hardly anything has changed for over a hundred years or more – has it?

◄
Victorian cabbies pose for the camera.
(J.B. Collection)

➤
'The 'Umming Bird', the all-electric Bersey, 1897. It had forty batteries of 80 volts each strapped under the body. It was probably the first mechanically-propelled car in the world. (J.B. Collection)

In 1897 probably the very first mechanically propelled cab in the world arrived on the streets of London. The Bersey electric-powered vehicle was a monstrous two-seater coupé, weighing 14 cwt and propelled by forty accumulator cells carried in a tray under the body that could propel the cabs for around 40 miles before it having to be recharged. They had a top speed of just 9mph. Despite replacing them the following year with a supposedly updated version capable of a top speed of 12mph, the Berseys were removed from service soon after because they kept breaking down and the cabbies refused to drive them.

In 1903 the first internal combustion engine cab, the Prunel, appeared. Other well-known manufacturers soon followed and by the end of 1906 makes such as Vauxhall, Ford, Herald, Rational, Argyll, Unic, Brasier, Marple, Pullcar and Humber had been licensed. New Conditions of Fitness for motor cabs were introduced in the same year and the fate of the horse-drawn cabs was sealed.

Horse bus and Renault cab, 1908.
(J.B. Collection)

Did you know?
The very last horse-drawn Hackney carriage licence was surrendered on 3 April 1947.

Did you know?

Rear-view mirrors in London taxis became a legal requirement as late as 1968. Even then they were secured firmly to the bulkhead and couldn't be adjusted. It was alleged that the authorities didn't want nefarious cabbies ogling the legs of their lady passengers! The guys used to joke that the mirrors were perfect for spotting low-flying planes and pigeons!

In 1903 there were over 11,000 horse-drawn cabs on the streets of London, 7,449 Hansom cabs and 3,905 Growlers. Within the short space of ten years leading up to the First World War, the number of Hansom cabs were reduced to 386 with just 1,547 Growlers remaining. Despite the Hansom cab being the most popular vehicle ever used by the cab trade, its days were numbered and within a decade these wonderfully designed vehicles were being broken up for firewood and sold at one shilling a bag!

The arrival of 500 Renaults in March 1907, operated by the General Motor Cab Co. Ltd, set the scene for a fierce debate and the company was severely criticised for 'going foreign'. This was the largest single order placed at that time anywhere in the world for a motor vehicle. The two-seater Renaults were virtually the same as those working in Paris and were fitted with a two-cylinder, 8–9hp engine and three-speed gearbox. But 'the London General' had invested heavily and they didn't want to be screwed by the wily cabbies. They refused to put their fleet of Renaults on the road until taximeters were made compulsory. French-built taxis were now dominating the London market. After the Renaults, there followed Unics, Darracqs, De Dion-Boutons, Brouhots and Vinots.

It's strange to relate, but some fifty years later Welbeck Motors launched their fleet of red Renault Dauphine mini-cabs on to the streets of London and very nearly destroyed the historic London taxi trade (by unlawfully touting on the streets) in one fell swoop!

◄
The Renault 1906, the car that caused all the furore among MPs with accusations of 'going foreign!' (J.B. Collection)

Did you know?
Taximeters were not made compulsory until late 1907.

➤

A vintage Unic from 1907. (Taxi Newspaper Collection)

➤➤

The Herald of 1906. (J.B. Collection)

Did you know?

Roof signs on taxis first appeared in 1910.

LD-3366

1907 UNIC TAXI

The Unic Taxi - seen here at full size - is one of the 1984 introductions in the Models of Yesteryear range.

These taxis were manufactured between 1904 and 1921 and this particular vehicle operated on the streets of London up to 1931. It was possible to hire it for as little as 3d.

Apart from its starring role in the Models of Yesteryear range, the taxi has featured in Whitehead Newsreel, Upstairs, Downstairs, The Forsythe Saga, etc. etc.

On loan from the London Cab Co.

➤
*The 1905 Vauxhall
attempting to emulate
the Hansom cab.
(J.B. collection)*

➤➤
*The Humber of 1908.
(J.B. Collection)*

Other new companies, looking for a piece of the action, followed the General Motor Cab Co. and soon there was a plethora of different types of taxis to be had. Some thirty-eight different motor manufacturers had vehicles working as taxis in London between 1903 and 1914.

However, it was patently obvious that all of these different vehicles wouldn't stand the test of time and be able to compete in the same market. And so it proved. By the outbreak of the First World War many of the companies had already gone out of business. Their costs had increased annually, but without the increased taxi fares, which were controlled by Parliament, going up accordingly. In fact taxi fares remained static from 1907 until 1920.

51

MILITANT LONDON CABBIES

The failure by the government to give a much-needed fare increase for thirteen years to the financially ailing cab trade, proved to be disastrous. The then Home Secretary Winston Churchill had flatly refused a final plea from fleet owners and proprietors. So, in a desperate attempt to offset their increasing and crippling costs, they took it upon themselves to demand all

➤
Cabbies and their families demonstrating in Kennington Park during the strike of 1913. (J.B. Collection)

the extras on the meter from the cabbies. However, the extras put on the meter for extra passengers and luggage had always been sacrosanct to the cabbies and were an integral part of their income.

So in 1912 the cabbies' union called a strike. This bitter strike had massive and total support from all London cabbies and the thousands of ancillary workers in the trade. Mass demonstrations were held regularly in Kennington Park almost opposite the largest cab garage in London, the General Motor Cab Co. Ltd – known to all cabbies as 'The London General'. This bitter strike finally came to an end later in the year when the Court of Arbitration found in favour of the taxi drivers. But later in the same year yet another cabbies' strike ensued when the price of petrol rose by 70 per cent. The fleet owners again made a mess of this issue by announcing that as from 1 January 1913, the drivers would have to pay the full amount of the increase which would in effect mean a 20 per cent cut in their earnings! This second strike went on for three months until some of the big fleet owners – desperate to have some money coming in before they went bankrupt – did private deals with the union to accept an offer of some five pence a gallon under the original asking price. The outcome was the inevitable break up of the large cab fleets, with the exception of a few, and led in the future to a collection of smaller proprietors and owner-drivers.

With the benefit of hindsight some may blame the various Home Secretaries for the two bitter strikes. Some may blame the large proprietors for being so money-grabbing, while others may lay the blame

Did you know?

In taxi slang an owner-driver is known as a 'mush' or 'musher'. It is said to derive from the early Gallic influence in the trade and is used in the same context as a French Canadian fur trapper willing his dog team to keep going by yelling out, 'mush, mush!' It's a good story – even if it is questionable!

on the cabbies for being too intransigent. Nevertheless, it became a benchmark for the solidarity and militancy of the trade throughout the ensuing years. There were 'drive-ins' and meetings when the government failed to take action against the unlicensed mini-cabs all through the 1960s. And in the late 1970s, literally hundreds of taxis completely blocked Whitehall protesting about the lack of a fare increase for three years. I remember that well because I had just won the prestigious Taxi Driver of the Year Competition and was invited to join leading trade figures and deliver the cabbies' petition to No. 10 Downing Street.

London cabbies have continued to express their willingness to protect their living against any unfair practices through the ages. So it's imperative that every new driver coming into our trade joins a trade organisation. Perhaps we should take a leaf out of our French brethren's book – when the Paris taxi drivers go out on strike, it's a 100 per cent walkout and not one single taxi goes to work!

◄
A mock execution of a 'Black Leg', Kennington Park, during the 1913 cabbies' strike. (J.B. Collection)

After the First World War there was an acute shortage of cabs in London for obvious reasons and these were hard times for everyone in the cab trade. The numbers of cabs were some 3,000 down on the 1914 figure and there were far more drivers than cabs. A new cab was urgently required to sort out the chaos and the introduction of the Mk I Beardmore, which was made in Paisley, Scotland, made things a lot easier.

The Beardmore Series, which included the Mk II (Super) in 1924 and the Mk III (Hyper) in 1929, proved to be most popular of all the cabs on the market until the arrival of the Austin series in the 1930s. Even so, there were still plenty of makes to choose from including the Mepward, Citroën, Fiat, Morris Commercial and Unic KF1. The Citroëns, which were introduced in 1923, were largely operated by the London General Cab Company. Following an edict by the Public Carriage Office in 1908 'banning passengers from sitting alongside the driver as with the early two-seater cabs,' any cabs built after 1908 had to be four-seaters forcing all the major cab companies to spend enormous amounts of money in converting their existing two-seater cabs.

The 1920s and '30s were hard times for the cab trade with low fares and the big depression. By the early 1930s Lord Ashfield became Chairman of the London Omnibus Company. He was also Chairman of the London Passenger Transport Board and the Traffic Advisory Committee. He became public enemy number one to all London cabbies by trying to clear cabs off the streets in favour of buses.

➤
The Beardmore
Mk I, the first taxi to be
manufactured after the
First World War, in 1919.
(J.B. Collection)

The Beardmore
Mk II in the 1920s.
*(Taxi Newspaper
Collection)*

➤➤
*Argyll taxis, c. 1921.
(Taxi Newspaper
Collection)*

RE?
OIL, GREASE & PARTS FOR
CARS, LORRIES & VANS
Of Every Description
ALWAYS for SALE or EXCHANGE

◄◄
A 1920s cabbie.
(The Jewish Museum
Collection)

◄
The popular Austin
'Low Loader' ,1934.
(J.B. Collection)

AGC 937

◀◀
A vintage 'Low Loader'
with a modern FX4.
(J.B. Collection)

◀
Attempting the PCO
'drive' in an old Austin
taxi. (J.B. Collection)

It was Lord Ashfield's Home Counties and London Traffic Advisory Committee which framed draconian new regulations attempting to put a stranglehold on taxis.

Disgruntled cabbies on demonstrations were heard to shout, 'Oxford Street is not Ashfield Avenue!' The way forward for the stable design of London taxis really began when Austin entered the market in the 1930s with the 'High Lot', which was based on the 'Heavy 12' saloon car. It wasn't long before they cornered the market and by 1937, out of 755 new cabs sold, 659 were Austins!

After the High Lot, Austin produced the Low Loader in 1934, so called because of the lowered floor pan. The Low Loader proved to be the most popular cab up until the outbreak of the Second World War. Then came the 'Flash Lot', so called because of its then ultra-modern styling, followed by the FX3 in 1948 and the FX4 in 1959.

The very first motor cab driver was a Mr James Howe of Wellesley Road, Hammersmith. In 1933 he was presented with a special badge by Lord Trenchard, the then Commissioner of Police.

◄◄
The modern Asquith taxis styled on the Austin 'High lot' of the 1930s. (London Vintage Taxi Association Collection)

Did you know?
The modern Asquith cab is styled on the old Austin High Lot. There are only eleven Asquiths plying for hire in London out of a fleet in excess of 22,000, and no more are being produced!

◄
Passing the PCO driving test in a 1920s Unic. (J.B. Collection)

◀◀
A Citroën, 1923. (J.B. Collection)

◀
A Morris-Commercial G type of 1929 alongside another taxi of the same period. (J.B. Collection)

Did you know?

The FX4, along with the Mini, became one of the longest-lived of British car designs. It was in production for thirty-eight years from 1959 right up until 1997, when the TX1 came into production.

internal combustion engine ... ly took over from the horse. ... is a taxi-cab rank in ... on, 1929.

◀
A taxi rank of Beardmores, 1929. (Taxi Newspaper Collection)

69

At the outbreak of the Second World War, the country was ill-prepared with the essential services well under strength. Their main weaknesses were a lack of manpower and sufficient vehicles to cover civilian emergencies should London be attacked from the air – and they knew it would be!

The obvious choice for a sturdy vehicle was the purpose-built London taxi that could be converted into just about anything they wanted it to be. So the government requisitioned around 2,500 taxis to be converted into auxiliary firefighting engines, ambulances and Army personnel carriers. The majority of their drivers volunteered to go with them for a wage of £3 a week! It was far from a cushy way of spending the war, because when the terrible London Blitz started, these cabs were in the thick of it. The cabbies, not fit enough for the armed forces but fit enough to drive a cab, had been trained by the professional firefighters. This firefighting outfit was called the AFS, the Auxiliary Fire Service, and specialised in dealing with small blazes deep in the narrow back streets of the capital. Because of their detailed knowledge of London, these cabs were often at the scene of a blaze well before the bigger engines arrived. Cabbies were mature under fire, many of them having seen service in the First World War. Other cabbies, too old to serve, carried on their profession right through to the end of the war. The trade was asked to form its very own Home Guard units and drivers, garage staff and owners willingly gave their time, skills and services. Petrol was strictly rationed, just enough to do a day's work, but the cabbies caused more controversy because they were only interested in short fares to save their fuel. When the GIs arrived in London with plenty of dough in their pockets, the cabbies were fiercely criticised for favouring them!

In the book *London Taxis at War*, my old mate, ex-cabbie Bill Eales recalls:

. . . in spite of the criticism levelled at cabbies, there was a group of taxi-men called the Biggin Hill Association. These guys made themselves available to the men of the Royal Air Force based at the famous fighter station in southern England, and would get the pilots back to their base after a night out in the west end of London. I am not absolutely sure, but I don't think they made any charge, which was a very nice gesture under the circumstances!

When the war ended and the boys came home, many of them went back to driving a taxi and life slowly returned to normal. Shortly after the war, Beardmore Motors marketed the popular Morris-Oxford Series 1, 2 and 3. Then came the Austin FX3 in 1948, one of the most popular taxis of all time with the cabbies that dominated the market. This was funded jointly by Carbodies of Coventry and Mann and Overton. In 1982, following the success of the famous

▲
An Austin taxi adapted for firefighting in the Second World War. (Taxi Newspaper Collection)

➤
Advertising the Morris-Commercial taxi.
(J.B. Collection)

➤➤
The prototype Austin FX3, 1948.
(J.B. Collection)

An Experience to Ride In! –

THAT'S THE NEW

MORRIS

COMMERCIAL

"SIX"

EARLY DELIVERY GUARANTEED.

STUDY THESE FEATURES:

"SIX" 6 cyl. 15 h.p. £37

ATTRACTIVE HIRE-PURCHASE TERM WITH BONUS FOR PROMPT PAYMEN ON APPLICATION

WATSON & CO. (L'pool) LTD.
GROSVENOR ROAD, LONDON, S.W.1

VICTORIA 7235/6

FX4 in 1958, London Taxis International bought the production rights from Austin and built the Fairway – an improved version of the FX4. The Beardmore Mark VII, the last of this famous line before the company ceased production in 1969, was launched in 1954. 1963 saw the arrival of the Winchester Mk 1 followed by the Mk 2 and the Mk 3, but none of these models are around today. Other prototype taxis never made it on to the production line.

An FX3 passing
Buckingham Palace.
(J.B. Collection)

Did you know?

The FX3 had hydraulic jacks that could be operated from outside the cab. Many were the times I left a cabbies' shelter late at night, started her up, put her into gear and went exactly nowhere. And why? Because one of the jokers had jacked it up while I was indoors!

Did you know?

More than 75,000

FX4s were built.

The London cab trade has provided passengers at Heathrow Airport with an excellent, personalised transport service for over half a century. In the bad old days, the flow of taxis at Heathrow depended on the whims and vested interests of small, tightly-knit groups of cabbies who organised themselves into cartels, or gangs. If my memory serves me right I believe one 'firm' was called the Quality Street Gang and another was known as the Lavender Hill Mob. If you weren't a 'face' and didn't belong to one of these 'firms', quite simply, you couldn't get on the only taxi rank in operation at that time. When one cab got hired, they would leave a space in the middle, only pulling forward when another 'face' arrived. Consequently all the 'Connaughts' (Connaught Rangers – strangers), were forced to continually orbit, that is to circle the airport hoping eventually to find a ranking space!

It was patently obvious to all concerned that a fast-growing international airport like Heathrow couldn't possibly function in a professional manner with a taxi operation like the one then in place. After dozens of complaints from influential passengers, BAA was forced into coming up with a fair and sensible solution. After many failed attempts, they finally utilised some spare space on the Northern Perimeter Road and erected a purpose-built Taxi Feeder Park.

'The licensed taxi trade is an integral part of the airport's ongoing transport plans.'

A senior BAA executive.

➤

Heathrow Airport in 1946. (Author's Collection)

➤➤

In 1946 a temporary tented village was erected at Heathrow. The onus was on building runways! (Author's Collection)

But BAA wanted to levy a small charge on every taxi using the new feeder park to recover their costs. That's when the trouble started. The levy may only have been a miserly 50p, but the cabbies and their trade organisations refused point-blank to pay any sort of charge, believing they were supplying an important service for BAA's passengers. The ensuing bitter strike lasted for over two months, but after a shattering statement from a senior trade figure, it eventually crumbled and the cabbies were forced to eat humble pie and pay up.

Many of the wiser old heads in the trade realised that the nominal 50p charge might well be the thin end of the wedge and they were spot-on; the charge for every cab to enter the Feeder Park now stands at £5.50. But the cabbies can recover some of the charge by putting £2 on the meter as extras, so the poor old passengers have to pay again!

> 'Whatever the result of the judicial review,
> I will instruct my members to return to work.'
>
> From the leader of one of the biggest trade unions,
> prior to the result of the impending judicial review.

An artist's impression of the new Terminal 5 at Heathrow.
(Author's Collection)

Cabs wait patiently in the taxi feeder park at Heathrow. (Author's Collection)

➤

And still the cabs wait at Heathrow. (Author's Collection)

Since those far-off days of the early 1990s, yet another purpose-built taxi feeder park has been constructed capable of holding around 500 cabs.

This time around, the fully-computerised system has eliminated all the various possible fiddles, and cabbies using this facility know full well that they will be called over to the Central Area in strict order. It's taken an awful long time, but BAA have finally got it right!

Individually the regular Heathrow cabbie is a pleasant enough person, but collectively they can become aggressive and volatile. They tend to stick together and distance themselves from the 'town' cabbies. But they certainly look after their own and the generous collections they make regularly for their sick friends and charities are legendary throughout the trade.

The airport regular is as sharp as a razor with a wicked sense of humour. You are given a nickname early on for a variety of reasons. Maybe it's where you live like, 'Bagshot' Bill, 'Hounslow' Ted, 'Ashford' 'Arry, or 'Gillingham' Jim. Perhaps it's about your physical features like, 'Banana Nose', or 'Wing-Nuts' (ears that stick out), or 'Flipper' (dodgy feet), Lenny 'Shoulders', or Ted 'The Neck'. I got stuck with Alf 'The Pipe' and because of my journalistic leanings, often it was 'Scoop'! And even your attire could get you a nickname as with, 'Woolly Hat' George, or John 'The Hat' and Fred 'The Suit'. Then you had the guys who resembled actors on the TV like, 'The Milky Bar Kid', 'Emmerdale', or 'Brains', as in *Thunderbirds*. Then we have 'The Muppet', or 'Joe 90' and 'Emu'. Perry 'Kettles' is so called because he mends

watches; 'Kettle is cockney rhyming slang for 'kettle and hob' (fob watch). Where your parents originated from is another source for nicknames; there's Mick 'The Greek' and George 'The Greek', 'Italian' Tony and 'Italian' Vic, 'Scotch' John, 'Welsh' Bob and 'Manchester' Ted. Even your previous job conjures up a nickname with Fred 'The Fireman', Ron 'The Dust' (as in dustman), 'The Coalman', Danny 'The Docker', 'Postman' Pat, John 'The Fish' (fishmonger), Sid 'The Grocer'. We even have 'Sheepdog' (shaggy hair and beard), 'The Jolly Green Giant' and 'Karate' Larry. Your driving also warrants a nickname at Heathrow as in Chrissy 'Hot Wheels', or 'The Motorway Mouse'. Then there's the way you eat and your eating habits; 'Knives and Forks' is eating all of the time, while 'Bread Roll' Mick has a bread roll with

everything! One of my favourite nicknames applies to this guy who can never back a winner, never gets a good fare and never wins at cards. He's a lovely guy but the nickname of 'Suffering' Peter is so very appropriate!

London cabbies working at Heathrow don't necessarily live in London and in many instances, not even in the UK. Quite a few live in Spain, Portugal, France and elsewhere on the Continent. 'Maltese' Arthur does two months at Heathrow then retires to his villa in Malta for the next two months. Johnny 'Mack' bought a place in Thailand and often comes over to work at 'the flyers'. 'Florida' John has got a place in West Palm Beach and spends six months here and six months there! Some of these guys crash out in their cabs overnight in the feeder park after an exhausting day's work and they are known as 'sleepers'. One of the best known of the 'sleepers' had the nickname of 'Mr Pastry'. Legend had it that he actually used to cook his breakfast on a Primus Stove in the back of his cab!

THE MYSTERIES OF CAB LANGUAGE

Cab language has evolved over many, many years and it's mixed with a large helping of cockney slang and racetrack slang. Some of the Heathrow slang is fairly obvious like a 'wrong 'un' (a dodgy job), a 'local' (going just outside the airport), a 'roader' (that's going a long way up the road), an 'in and out', (that's returning with the same passenger) and 'outside the Met', means a fare wanting to go outside the Metropolitan Police District, which is a negotiated price.

The cab language in London is truly a language all of its own. This is a typical day in the life of a Cockney cabbie. You get up bright and early sometimes, a quick bite to eat then upstairs to wash your 'boat' (boat race – face), brush the 'Hampsteads' (Hampstead Heaths – teeth) and comb the remnants of your 'Barnet' (Barnet Fair – hair). Then on with your 'Dicky' (Dicky Dirt – shirt), your 'strides' (trousers) and your 'Almonds' (Almond Rocks – socks) and 'St Louis' (St Louis Blues – shoes). Put on your badge, pick up your 'float' (money bag), a quick kiss on the cheek for the 'Trouble and Strife' (wife), then down the 'Apples' (Apples and Pears – (stairs) to the garage. The wind is blowing a gale and it really is 'Taters' (Taters in the Mould – cold); please God the 'sherbet' (sherbet dab – cab) turns over and starts! After much coughing and

spluttering, it eventually fires into life, so you switch on the 'hickory' (hickory-dickory-dock – clock/taximeter) and hope to God that you can find a fare because it's the 'Kipper Season' (when the trade is slack in January, February and March). Nobody really knows where this saying originated, some believe it's because the trade is as flat as a kippper; others say it comes from Victorian times when the cabbies had to eat kippers because they were so poor! Your first job could be a 'single-pin' (one passenger), or a 'bowler-hat' (a City gent). Maybe it's a couple, known to us as ('im and 'er), or a 'three-' or 'four-hander'. Hopefully you wouldn't have picked up a 'bilker' (someone who does a runner without paying the fare and a person you should have 'broomed' (refused) in the first place).

If your luck is out your first passenger may 'legal you off' (giving the legal fare with no tip). The tourists, no doubt, will want 'the Wedding Cake' (the Queen Victoria Memorial Monument in front of Buckingham Palace), while the 'Bowler Hat' might require 'Pill Avenue' (Harley Street) or 'The Gasworks' (the Houses of Parliament)! Many of the mainline stations have nicknames; 'Padders' is (Paddington), 'The Vic' (Victoria), 'The Loo' (Waterloo) and 'The Liver' (Liverpool Street). Then we have 'The Rocking Horse' (Kings Cross) and 'The Pancake' (St Pancras).

If you are working days, you normally have a count-up at lunchtime and anything more than a 'pony', (twenty-five pounds), is not bad going. Maybe you've had a 'result' – a blinding long fare and you've earned a 'nifty' (fifty quid). If so, then you're looking for a 'wunner' (a hundred pounds), before you end your shift, but this is far from the norm. Yet with all my many years of experience, it still fascinates me to hear the 'success stories' when I visit a cabbies' shelter for a cuppa. I often think I'm doing a totally different job from many of these guys I listen to. Maybe it's just a case of one-upmanship when they bang on about earning a 'bottle' (two hundred pounds), or even a 'carpet' (three hundred pounds)! Nevertheless I still enjoy hearing these tales and the way they are told – talk about stand-up comedy, they're brilliant!

Any new driver coming into the trade is known as a 'Butterboy'. Many cabbies believe this means 'but-a-boy', while others think it means 'taking the butter – the cream' from their children. In fact it originates from Victorian times when many London cabbies lived in the country. During the summer, 'the busy period', they would come up to town and work like dogs for the whole season. The regular cabbies objected to these part-timers, saying they'd arrive in the summer and disappear again in the winter, just like 'bleedin' butterfies'. Over the years this disparaging nickname has changed into 'Butterboy' to mean a new face.

Did you know?

Another Cockney rhyming slang name for a cab is 'Lobster' – as in lobster and crab.

Did you know?

It is an offence for a cabbie not to wear his badge 'on his right breast', as the Act instructs, during the hours of his employment!

◄

Cabbie Del McCarrick with Carol Vorderman. Del puts on his Roger Rabbit costume and runs sponsored marathons all over the world. He has raised over £100,000 for Leukaemia Research and has just received the MBE! (Taxi Newspaper Collection)

I finally finished The Knowledge and earned my coveted Green Badge just before Christmas 1962. The FX4 had been on the road since 1958, but there were still many FX3s still working as they had been since 1948. I enjoyed driving the FX3, even though with just a sliding window facing out to the luggage compartment, it was absolutely freezing cold in the winter and the old-fashioned, rod braking system left a lot to be desired. Some FX3s veered to the right when braking, while others veered to the left. But it didn't take too long to work out the vagaries of my particular FX3 – because if I didn't, it meant a day or more in the garage waiting for them to knock out the dents!

At that time, the licensed taxi trade in London was in turmoil. Welbeck Motors, the very first unlicensed mini-cab company to challenge our virtual monopoly, had been backed financially to the tune of £1 million. They 'acquired' the services of two MPs to ask 'friendly' questions on their behalf in the House.

One of the MPs on Welbeck's 'payroll' tabled a motion in the house saying, quite incorrectly, that, 'London cabs are unable

A Welbeck Renault mini-cab in the early 1960s. (With thanks to Stanley Roth)

to meet the needs of the public,' and suggested, 'the introduction of mini taxis and motorised rickshaws which would require Home Office approval.' It's worth noting that this question was asked seven months before the first Renault Dauphine took to the streets of London! Having failed to gain the Government's open approval, the campaign was switched to a more receptive channel, the press.

Carbodies of Coventry
FX4 production line,
1975. (J.B. Collection)

➤➤
Taking delivery of two
FX4s. (Taxi Newspaper
Collection)

'Men of wealth have been heard to cry out against the taximeter – men who think nothing of signing away many thousands in seconds in the wiggle of a pen; but find it very painful to sit helplessly in the back of a taxi watching their money dripping away in three penny stages'.

The Times, 2 March 1961

The joke was really on the writer in *The Times*, because some sixty years earlier his paper had been at the forefront of a campaign for the introduction of the taximeter. However, The fleet of red Renaults hit the streets of London in 1961.

This bitter and often violent dispute between London cabbies and their unlicensed opposite numbers rumbled on for months. The cabbies were furious that this company was virtually flouting the law by literally driving a Renault Dauphine through the Private Hire Act. Then out of the blue many of the major players at Welbeck Motors resigned and in 1965, they went into liquidation with total liabilities of £50,000. It was heavily rumoured at the time that the millionaire Mr Isaac Wolfson, who had put most of the finance into place, had been told that

the bad press surrounding his mini-cab venture could well prejudice his coveted knighthood. Suffice to say, soon after he pulled the plug on Welbeck, he did indeed become Sir Isaac Wolfson and became famous for his philanthropic work. He died in 1991.

One MP who had lobbied for Welbeck and their backers, was left stranded in the chamber when they all departed from the scene. All he could do now to hide his embarrassment was to make fun of the situation by saying, 'It is high time the winds of change blew through the Public Carriage Office, it was festooned with cobwebs, strewn with horse manure and had an all-pervading smell of horses. The London cab trade wanted a monopoly and a scarcity of cabs.' It is alleged he sat down amid jeers from the members!

➤➤

Sid James and Charles Hawtrey on the set of the 1963 film Carry on Cabby. *(London Vintage Taxi Association Collection)*

Sadly this was far from the end of the mini-cab saga for the London cabbies – in fact it was just the beginning! Many shrewd and interested parties watching from the wings now realised that it was quite possible to bypass the stringent Hackney Carriage Laws and easily create a second-tier, back street 'taxi' service! And so these scruffy mini-cab offices started to proliferate all over London; hiring, in many instances, drivers with past

➤

LTI works, Coventry. (J.B. Collection)

Did you know?

In 1973 the government imposed VAT on the cab
trade, the only passenger-carrying industry to suffer
this imposition. Today, VAT accounts for over £2,000
of the price of a new taxi!

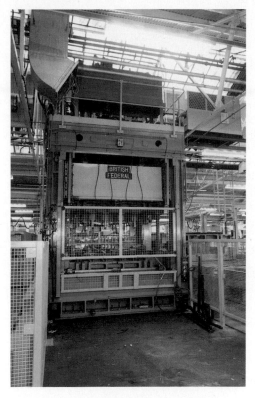

criminal records of rape and violence. The cars being used by these illegal touts were often dangerous and absolute 'rust-buckets', but nobody seemed to care. Only now, after more than forty years and many cases of assault, is it being finally recognised that women getting into the cars of unlicensed touts are in grave danger. Full credit must be given to former Mayor of London Ken Livingstone for organising a special task force to combat the many taxi-touts that roamed Soho every night. It's just a shame that it has taken this long to achieve.

After driving an FX3 with dodgy brakes for a few years, I decided to treat myself to the brand-new four-door Beardmore, just on the market. Unfortunately the company suddenly went bust in 1969 after fifty years of manufacturing quality, coach-built cabs – before my name came up for delivery, so

I purchased an FX4. The price of an FX4 in the late 1960s was around £1,200 – on the never-never of course. Now some forty years on, the new TX4 is around £32,000 – plus hire purchase charges!

During the 1970s, because of the closure of the Royal Docks and all the national papers moving out of Fleet Street after the defeat of the powerful print unions, there was a tremendous influx of guys doing The Knowledge. These young cabbies, when they eventually got their badge, were a totally different breed than the older cabbies who had been in the game for many years. They worked much longer hours, they didn't want to sit and natter in cab shelters for many of them weren't in the least bit interested in joining unions or trade organisations. Yet just a few short years before, you needed to be a member of the Transport & General Workers' Union (Cab Section) to hire a cab from an East End garage! Another reason – and a major factor for fragmenting trade unity – was the introduction of the 'flat-rate' system. Way back from the start of the taxi trade it had always been the norm for the driver to share

◄◄
The TX1 final assembly line. (Author's Collection)

▼
New jigs for the TX1. (Author's Collection)

◀◀
Cabbies check out the new TX1. (Author's Collection)

◀
The new TX1, known affectionately as 'The Noddy Car' by London cabbies. (Author's Collection. LTI Limited reproduced with permission. Fairway and TX shape is a registered design. Fairway^{TM}, TX^{TM}, the LTI Device, the LTI logo and the London Taxis International logo are all trademarks of LTI Limited.)

a percentage of the meter with his guv'nor and keep his extras and tips. Now with the 'flat-rate' system, the driver hired the cab for a whole week at a set rate. He was expected to put in his own diesel and oil and keep the cab clean. Consequently, the driver didn't have to go back to his garage every day of the week to pay in, so all the cab-washers

The 'Classic' edition from Mann & Overton. (Author's Collection. LTI Limited reproduced with permission. Fairway and TX shape is a registered design. Fairway™, TX™, the LTI Device, the LTI logo and the London Taxis International logo are all trademarks of LTI Limited.)

Did you know?

Beardmore only managed to produce THREE of their new four-door vehicles before they went bust. These three cabs are now worth a lot of money in the vintage cab market!

– and many of the mechanics – became surplus to requirements. In fact the drivers of these cabs 'on the flat', were hardly seen by anyone anymore. All these guys wanted to do was get out on the road for as long as they could and not get involved in anything to do with the trade. So when the trade organisations needed total support in their fight against unlicensed mini-cabs, they discovered to their cost that many cabbies weren't in the least bit interested! Sad to say, but many cabs were still plying for hire while thousands of their fellow workers were involved in demos and drive-ins!

◀
A TX1 posing on Westminster Bridge. (Author's Collection)

Did you know?
Exterior advertising on taxis has only been permitted since 1990.

Working on FX4s at
Carbodies, Coventry.
(J.B. Collection)

THE METROCAB

Metro-Cammell-Weyman launched the Metrocab in 1987 and it passed through four owners, the most successful being Hooper, until Kamkorp, its last owner, pulled the plug on the company in April 2006.

I have been the proud owner of a Metrocab for the past twelve years and despite jibes from other cabbies that 'they

The author advertising his first book, Cabbie. *(Author's Collection)*

look like a bleedin' hearse', I'm very fond of them and sad that the company has gone out of business. I like the fibreglass body that doesn't suffer from rust and I like the reliable Ford Transit 2.5-litre engine that doesn't require any oil from one month to the next. But even at the very peak of their sales the Metrocab could only attain around 11 per cent of the taxi market, so they found it very hard to compete with LTI (London Taxi International). But the Toyota-powered 'TTT', their latest model before they went bust would, I believe, have challenged the might of LTI. This was a super cab and is still much sought after.

Nevertheless, their untimely demise once again brings up the old 'chestnut' of LTI's monopoly in the market place. Many cabbies are saying that without any competition LTI can charge just about any price they want to for their product and, if you don't like it, you'll just have to lump it! That's basically the reason for a groundswell of opinion opting for an alternative vehicle!

◄◄ *Building Metrocabs. (J.B. Collection)*

◄ *Metrocabs bound for Moscow. (Author's Collection)*

▲
HRH the Duke of Edinburgh takes delivery of his new Metrocab gas taxi. He used this vehicle for many years. (Author's Collection)

◄
The Queen and the Duke of Edinburgh try out the new 'green' gas Metrocabs. (Author's Collection)

With the licensing of mini-cabs in London – now given the more up-market name of Private Hire – the cab trade faces its biggest ever battle. Presently there are somewhere in the region of 53,000 in the process of being licensed and that's more than double the number of cabbies on the road. I've no doubt whatsoever there will be many more as the PHV companies get their act together. So what do we do to combat this threat against our livelihood – apart from burying our heads in the sand as in the past? In my opinion trade unity is the first consideration – because if we're not united we might just as well throw in the towel right away. But our problem stems from the fact that many of the new drivers coming into the trade are simply not interested in trade politics. Some of them are under the illusion that, because they've completed the Demon Knowledge, the world owes them a living! We've now reached the sorry state of affairs where less than one-third of London cabbies belong to any trade organisation. And sadly there doesn't appear to be a forum where all the trade organisations can sit down together and discuss the relevant issues. Instead they always seem to be squabbling among themselves, vying for top spot!

The differences between the two sides are plain to see if you possess just a wee bit of business acumen. Firstly the licensed cabbies with a history stretching back many centuries and driving a vehicle that is a global 'icon'; the drivers are professional and highly-trained but some of them now tend to be a bit choosy about certain destinations they are given. Hence one of the long-running jokes when a cabbie

Did you know?

Cabbies still have to abide by the laws laid down in the London Hackney Carriage Acts of 1831 and 1843. Among these antiquated laws are terms of one or two months' imprisonment for piddling offences like, 'misbehaviour during employment' and 'use of insulting or abusive gestures during employment'. It's a wonder there are any cabs left on the road!

▲
Me taking breakfast with Countess Spencer. (Author's Collection)

➤
1979. Cabbies demonstrate in Whitehall over no fare increase for three years. (Taxi Newspaper Collection)

is asked to go south of the Thames, 'I'm sorry guv', but I get a nose-bleed when I pass water!' The London cabbie is relaxed and comfortable in the knowledge that he is certainly the best taxi driver on the planet. But in that relaxed and comfortable knowledge he is in danger of becoming over-confident, or even slightly patronising

with what is basically a monopoly! I recall back in the 1960s when we all sat around in the cab shelters, clucking like old hens and telling each other that mini-cabs would never affect us. Slogans were bandied about like, 'punters in London will always want a licensed taxi' and 'we'll always get a good living.' Those slogans were basically as true in the 1960s as they are today. We did get a good living back then and we're still getting a good living today. But at what cost? I know of young cabbies who are working twelve or sometimes fourteen hours every day to earn wages comparable to what we earned some thirty years ago in half that amount of hours!

The bottom line is that any cake is only so big and now there are a lot more people having a nibble at it, so we as licensed cabbies are slowly but surely being

117

➤
Just another day at the office! (Author's Collection)

squeezed into an ever-decreasing area in Central London. The biggest problem as I see it is that we cabbies are all individuals operating one vehicle. We have our own times, own days of working and our own amount of hours we like to work. Not so private hire: they are told what time to start and what time to finish – and if you turn up late one morning, then you don't work that day! Unlike us they have shrewd bosses with lots of past business experience, who

'These restrictions lead to fewer taxis, higher fares, less suitable taxis for the needs of the disabled and the unavailability of safer and more comfortable taxis to the disadvantage in general of passengers and drivers alike.'

A barrister arguing his case for the benefit of a major car company wanting to break the monopoly of the purpose-built taxi. They lost the case. . .

run the fleets as profit-making concerns for their shareholders. So while many of us cabbies don't work weekends, Bank Holidays and the like, myself included, these PHV drivers are beavering away and capturing the profitable corporate accounts presently run by the licensed radio circuits. Many of us did The Knowledge in the first instance for the freedom of the job, but now we are being seriously challenged by major PHV companies who need to show a profit on their annual accounts. It's time we started learning from them; if we don't, then the future for the famous London cabbie could be in jeopardy!

Ever since the late 1960s when I first put pen to paper in the trade press, I have been a strong advocate of the purpose-built London taxi. Some may call me an old dinosaur, but my feelings on this subject

▲
The now-defunct Winchester taxi. (Taxi Newspaper Collection)

alternative vehicles like MPVs (multi-purpose vehicles) into the London taxi market, it will bring down prices considerably. Presently there has already been one legal challenge to the stringent 'Conditions of Fitness' from a major player in the MPV market. And, with a huge potential market, it is likely that many more will follow.

But after a lengthy and comprehensive review, the Public Carriage Office replied. 'The facts of these alleged disbeliefs were not borne out.' They decided to retain the 25ft turning circle which effectively thwarts any alternative vehicle entering the market – unless the manufacturers completely re-tool their assembly lines.

I can well understand the young cabbies just coming into the trade wanting to save around £10,000 by buying an MPV, instead of the slightly antiquated and (in the

have been well-documented from day one. Yet today, many in the trade are complaining bitterly that because of the monopoly by LTI (London Taxi International) – especially now Metrocab have gone under – the present vehicles are far too expensive at around £32,000. They argue that by allowing

opinion of many), over-priced, purpose-built taxi. But, without wanting to sound too melodramatic, I fervently believe our 'icon' is the last remaining ace against the opposition of our ever-diminishing, 350-year supremacy. The bottom line with us is the 'recognition factor' because visitors from all over the world know what a London taxi looks like. How would it be in the future if the only difference between us and the opposition was a 'For-Hire' sign and a taximeter adapted to a multi-purpose vehicle? Mark my words, it wouldn't take too long before the confused punters were hailing any MPV on the road and many an illegal taxi will stop to pick them up! Love it or loathe it, our purpose-built taxi is a world icon and consequently as London cabbies, so are we. Many of the new boys simply can't comprehend just how

famous we are. This is a classic example of the extraordinary impact the London taxi has on visiting tourists. A few years back I was tentatively involved with a major hotel chain when they conducted a massive survey right across the USA, asking potential visitors to London to list their top five 'wannadoes'. Top of the list

An early Metrocab, 1970. (J.B. Collection)

121

359 ELL

◄◄
An early Winchester,
1963. (J.B. Collection)

◄
A later model Winchester.
(London Vintage Taxi
Association Collection)

123

and way out on its own was, 'I wanna ride in a REAL London taxi'. A distant second was having an English breakfast of eggs and bacon! If the anti-purpose-built taxi lobby ever got their way, will the thousands of visiting tourists ever say they'd just *love* to have a ride in an MPV – while eating their eggs and bacon in the back? An old saying that comes to mind is, 'If it's not broke, don't try to fix it'!

Yet another quote allegedly coming from the powers that be with the announcement of London's successful Olympic bid was: 'With the arrival of millions of extra visitors in 2012 for The London Olympics, the taxi trade might not be able to cope. Maybe we could possibly allow PHVs to ply for hire – just during the Games – of course'.

And that possible scenario my friends will surely be game, set and match and see the eventual demise of our historic trade!

'London taxis are an integral part of the capital's transport system'.
Former Mayor Ken Livingstone